D1631757

Evening News

Images of Edinburgh

Evening News

Images of Edinburgh

The Breedon Books
Publishing Company
Derby

First published in Great Britain by
The Breedon Books Publishing Company Limited
44 Friar Gate, Derby, DE1 1DA
1993

© Edinburgh Evening News 1993

All Rights Reserved. No part of this publication may be
reproduced, stored in a retrieval system, or transmitted in any form,
or by any means, electronic, mechanical, photocopying, recording
or otherwise without the prior permission in writing of the
Copyright holders, nor be otherwise circulated in any form or
binding or cover other than in which it is published and without a
similar condition including this condition being imposed on the
subsequent publisher.

ISBN 1 873626 61 4

Printed and bound by Hillmans Printers, Frome, Somerset.
Covers printed by BDC Printing Services Limited of Derby.

Contents

Introduction

IT WAS an Englishman, the Revd Sydney Smith, who wrote of Edinburgh in 1798: "I like this place extremely and cannot help thinking that for a literary man, by which term I mean a man who is fond of letters, it has the most eligible situation in the island.

"It unites good libraries liberally managed, learned men without any other system than that of pursuing truth; very good general society; large healthy virgins, with mild pleasant countenances, and white swelling breasts . . .

"Some little defects, it has to be sure, but they are frivolous and ludicrous; one is, as you must have observed, a total want of all faecal propriety and excremental delicacy . . ."

Times have changed, and the smells of the Old Town have been tamed with modern sanitation. The cries of 'gardyloo' are no longer heard, as they once were, when slops were thrown from a window on to the street. But some things never change. Edinburgh is not one town, but two. Perhaps even three.

The Old Town is where it began with the castle on the rock and it spread downhill to what is now the Palace of Holyroodhouse. Over the centuries the city grew, huddled together for protection, but spilling out over the sides of the narrow ridge in closes, wynds and warrens.

It was a teeming mass of people piled high on top of one another with the gentry at the top and the lower social orders ranked beneath them.

Lives were lived, disasters occurred, fire caused particular havoc with so many wooden buildings, crimes were committed, riots took place, hangings, shootings, witches were burned, and people came back from the dead . . .

Mary, Queen of Scots, Bonnie Prince Charlie, James VI of Scotland, I of England, John Knox, have their stories to tell, as have a multitude of lesser-known citizens who have left their mark on history. Today, Edinburgh is a place full of legend and ghosts. There are stories of headless men and women, headless dogs and cats, secret passages and closes that have been closed for centuries.

Edinburgh is slow to change. When a building has been demolished it has often taken 20 years or more to replace it — such is the length of the argument that has gone on about the use the site should be put to. In the Old Town this dithering has been an advantage. Restoration is now the way forward, and if new buildings are needed, they must conform to the style of those around them.

This did not always happen, and the New Town, Edinburgh's other face, suffered in the Sixties when a number of elegant old buildings were pulled down to make way for modern architecture.

Fortunately, due in part to the city's procrastination, some of the worst ideas, such as a motorway cutting right through the city centre, never took place. Today, even the thought would be criminal.

The New Town is more than 200 years old, and is the home of Edinburgh's business community. Bankers, lawyers, insurance companies and financial houses abound in its busiest part, the stretch between St Andrew Square and Charlotte Square at each end of George Street. Ghosts probably survive here, too, but everyone is too busy to notice.

But the New Town does have its share of history. Robert Louis Stevenson lived here, as did Alexander Graham Bell, James Young Simpson, the discoverer of chloroform, Sir Compton Mackenzie, Arthur Conan Doyle and Rebecca West. The list of people associated with the New Town is endless. The Revd Sydney Smith lived at 38 Hanover Street.

Leith is the third face of Edinburgh. Today it is a thriving area, bursting with renovation. New ideas and new homes abound.

Ships and the sea are still important parts of the Leith story, but the days of the great whaling fleets are over. So are the steamers to London. Queues of seamen looking for ships have been replaced by yuppies looking for waterfront wine bars.

Leith's greatest export is probably golf. It is said that Leith Links was the world's first golf course, and that James VI played the game there before he went to England to become James I.

It has its own contribution to make to history too. Mary, Queen of Scots, landed here from France to take up her crown and stayed the night at Lamb's House, now an old folks' day centre, before proceeding to the capital.

John Paul Jones, the renegade British officer who founded the United States Navy, blockaded the port during the War of Independence.

Edinburgh is a city full of surprises and delights. Many people have echoed the words of the Revd Sydney Smith when he wrote: "I left Edinburgh with great heaviness of heart."

John Bennett
Edinburgh
June 1993

Princes Street

From the Old Town, the closes lead away from the Royal Mile on either side. To the north they run down to the valley that harbours Princes Street Gardens. Here, a glimpse through Advocate's Close reveals the Scott Monument standing sentinel on Princes Street.

It is August 1950 and the Castle broods over the city. A points policeman directs the traffic at the West End, and the tram cars indicate a less hectic age.

The West End was never this quiet, except perhaps on a Sunday morning. But here someone has stylish transport. The date was 4 May 1953.

Above and below: What a difference 67 years can make. The horse-drawn trams and the parasols belong to 1885, while the motor cars and the road works were going on in 1952.

Early this century when cable cars had taken over from the horse-drawn trams. On the right of the picture is the Royal Scottish Academy. In the far distance can be seen the Nelson Monument and the National Disgrace.

Princes Street from the top of the Scott Monument early this century. On the right is the roof of the old Waverley Market, and behind it the North British Hotel.

Gone . . .but not forgotten. R.W.Forsyth, one of the capital's more elegant department stores, closed its doors in 1981.
But the building still stands.

Thortons sports shop stood on the corner of Princes Street and Hanover Street.

Darling's, the ladies' fashion store that was as well-known for the idiosyncrasies of its owner as it was for fashion. During World War Two, Sir William Y. Darling was Lord Provost and he strutted about the city in RAF uniform. When he was in civilian clothes he was even more spectacular, in morning coat and top hat, and he beamed as he spoke to people he passed in the street. A genuine Edinburgh character.

Two views of the Life Association building, one at the turn of the century, the other in the mid-1960s, when it was about to be demolished to make way for modern architecture.

Maule's Corner at the West End. The shop was later to become Binn's, and now House of Fraser.

Even in 1909 shops closed down. Here Summers and McIntyre are giving up business on the corner of Princes Street and Castle Street.

Pomp and ceremony as the Scots Guards march along Princes Street. Taking the salute is Lord Provost Sir James Miller. The year was 1951.

The march past of the tram cars. In the early 1950s, motor cars were still not a major traffic problem, but the trams
sometimes came to a halt.

At the turn of the century things were different. Horses never seemed to cause traffic jams.

The Floral Clock in the Gardens. Probably the world's first, it was established in 1903 and has been copied many times. In 1951 it was commemorating the Festival of Britain.

Princes Street at night, and new illuminated decorations were being tried out in May 1962.

It is 1902 and the city turns out to welcome a detachment of Indian troops.

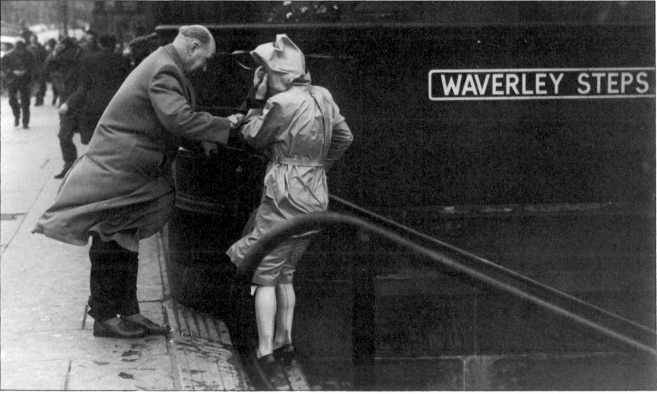

Edinburgh is rightly famed for its East wind, and the windiest place of all is at the top of the Waverley Steps. Here, in August 1956, a man and woman struggle against the elements.

1969 — a year of mini skirts and new letter boxes. This one was being tried out at the foot of Hanover Street. The Royal Scottish Academy is in the background and a part of the Castle lurks at the top right.

The East End, and the horse-drawn trams are outside the GPO in the 1890s. In November 1943 nothing much had changed except there were fewer horses. The Wellington statue is on the left. That particular horse, it is said, jumps to the pavement every time it hears the one-o-clock gun fired from the Castle.

A moment of tranquility at the East End at the turn of the century, and Wellington's horse is still on its pedestal.

Style and fashion in Princes Street around 1898.

A tram on its way to Leith, a horse bus from South Queensferry, this was travel in the 1880s.

The New Waverley Market, new buses and even some sunshine in Princes Street in the 1990s.

The Royal Mile

Edinburgh Castle in 1897.

The Castle stands high at the back of this picture of the Royal Mile looking west from the spire of the Tron Church. The spire of the High Kirk of St Giles is prominent in the centre.

The Royal Mile from the Tron looking East, and right in the centre of the picture is John Knox House, now a museum.
It was a sunny day in November 1955.

The turn of the century and this was Mylne's Court in the Lawnmarket.

Opposite Mylne's Court, the old Bow Head, also at the turn of the century.

Gladstone's Land in the Lawnmarket. In 1936, Ramages Dairy and the Robbie Burns bar held court, but it was in a house near here that Robert Burns stayed on his first visit to Edinburgh. The youthful Walter Scott met him at that time in Sciennes House. A momentous occasion for the young author-to-be.

Brodie's Close in the Lawnmarket in 1956. The entire corner was demolished to make way for new council buildings.

The Heart of Midlothian is figured out in granite setts on the street. It is claimed this is the site of the death cell in the old Tollbooth prison. This picture dates from the 1890s.

Matthew and Son were big in the drapery business around 1905, but nothing can halt progress and the whole block was demolished to make way for today's Sheriff court.

The Tron church in the early 1950s. The spire of St Giles can be seen in the background.

The High Street in April 1960 with the Tron and St Giles dominating the skyline.

Adam Brown, blinded, maimed and disfigured, stands at the pavement's edge in the High Street outside the Tron Kirk
at the end of last century. His placard declares: "He has no pension."

First there was Stewart Lamb, then there was Grants. This corner of the High Street and North Bridge has seen many changes. A large part of the building has now been converted into flats.

The side door of Patrick Thomson in the late 1950s. This was perhaps Edinburgh's largest department store. Gone now, the upper floors have been converted into a hotel.

Even last century there were antique dealers, and McCulloch's did a good line in up-to-the-minute furnishings as well.

In 1954 it was the smallest shop in the city, but two customers could squeeze in to seal a bargain in antiques.

The Canongate Tolbooth as it was last century and in the early 1950s. It was originally built in 1591 and was the meeting place of the Canongate Council. Today, it is a museum.

Central Edinburgh

A cannon stands guard over the city. This was the view from Calton Hill, looking down Princes Street in the mid-1950s.

Cockburn Street leading off the Royal Mile to Waverley Bridge and the railway station in the early 1960s. It is a one-way street now with an abundance of curio shops.

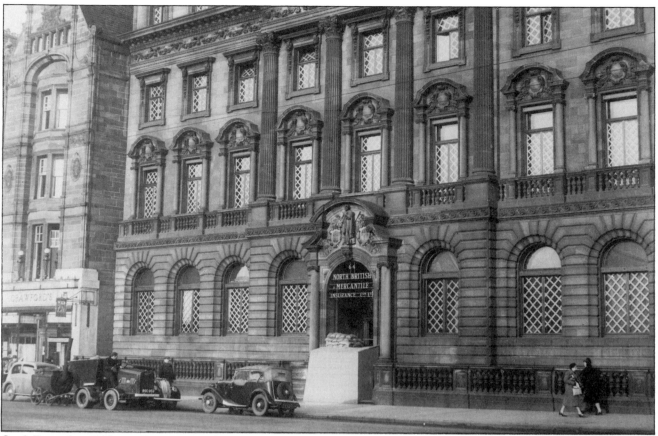

On 1 December 1939, sandbags at the door and taped windows indicate that the North British and Mercantile Insurance in Princes Street was ready for war.

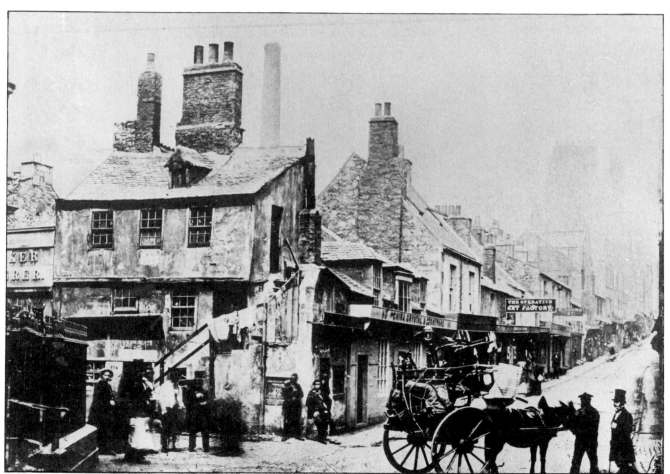

An office block is on this corner now, but about 1850, the foot of St Mary's Street was a clutter of small shops and homes. One man with a cart seems to moving all his possessions.

A loaf of bread for five pence was the special offer at the Bread and Potato Store off the Cowgate in 1866.

Still recognisable after more than a hundred years, this is the Cowgate at the arch of George IV Bridge looking towards the Grassmarket.

For around a thousand years a castle of some sort has looked down on the city that was at its feet. This is the view from the Grassmarket taken early in the century. In the centre is the Beehive Inn, still there today.

A mist hangs over the gardens and the skyline of the Old Town is silhouetted against a November sun in the mid-1950s.

They called them the Queen Street girls, and this was their school, Mary Erskine's, in Queen Street in the 1920s. The school has since moved to new buildings away from the city centre.

It is 12 January 1954, and this was the last tram to run from Corstorphine into the city on its way to Leith for the last round-up.

The early 1920s, on the junction of Hanover Street and George Street. No traffic moves and there is plenty of room for parking.

The Castle, the Usher Hall, Lothian Road and the square in front of the Sheraton Hotel. This is Edinburgh in the 1990s.

Celebration time . . .a fireworks display in the Meadows on 20 February 1960, to mark the birth the previous day of Prince Andrew.

Heart of Midlothian were taken to the heart of the city in 1956 when they won the Scottish Cup 3-1 against Celtic. It seemed the whole town turned out in Princes Street to welcome them home.

Fashion for men . . .and for £180 you could have had this coat from a Princes Street store in September 1958.

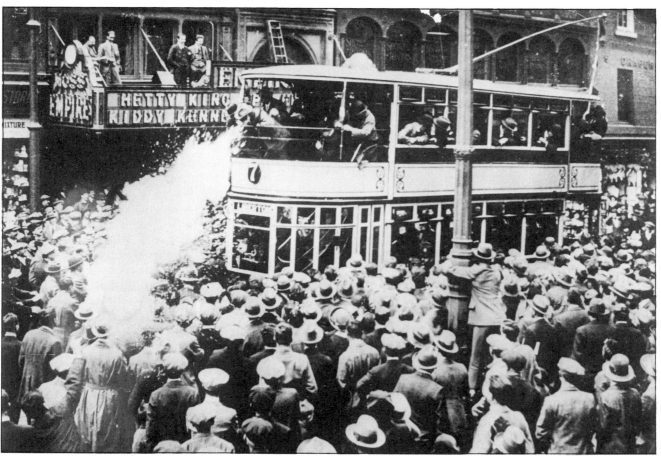

The first electric tram to run from Leith to Edinburgh. This one carried members of the Town Council, and was halted by students at the Empire Theatre and pelted with flour, soot, tomatoes and eggs. It was June 1922.

Edinburgh receives many visitors from the United States, but few of them travel on a bike. This one did, though, in August 1955, half-way through this attempt to cycle around the world.

The one-man band was a well-known city attraction in the 1950s and '60s. Here he brings music to Ramsay Garden.

A quiet moment in Inglis Bar at the top of Cockburn Street around 1900.

There was a bus strike in July 1957, and almost everyone wanted to travel by train.

John Knox looks down sympathetically on the driver who seems to have fallen asleep in his car outside the Assembly Hall in 1962.

February 18 1955, and this was the scene in Lothian Road just before it joins Princes Street.

The Calton Hill, and washer women lay out their whites to be bleached in the sun outside the observatory late last century.

This was the Sheriff Court in 1931 before it moved to its present site. This building, in George IV Bridge, was demolished to make way for the National Library of Scotland.

A dreich day in November 1954. The wind and the rain blowing off the North Sea can make a chilly combination. This is North Bridge, leading down to the East End of Princes Street.

Poole's Synod Hall was a monster of a building. It contained a cinema, meeting rooms for a number of societies and a public rifle range. It was pulled down in 1965 to become one of the capital's notorious gap sites for many years. It has now been used for an office block.

The Castle taken from Spittal Street at the turn of the century, with Johnston Terrace winding around the rock.

You could get four per cent interest on your deposits with Farrow's Bank in the latter part of last century.

Crowds gathered, an awning was erected, flags were flying, when the foundation stone was laid for the new North Bridge on 25 May 1896.

Construction work continues on the North Bridge.

In 1901, the bridge is finished, but work goes on to build the North British Hotel.

The roof of the Waverley Market at the end of last century. The building in the background was demolished to make way for the North British Hotel.

The old Calton Jail taken in 1930. This building was swept away to be replaced by St Andrew's House, the seat of government in Scotland, but the Governor's house on the far left of the picture, remains.

A view from the front of the Calton jail.

St Andrew's House, photographed from under the North Bridge. On the left of the building the governor's house still stands. In the centre of the picture Nelson's Column stands out on top of Calton Hill.

The gateway to Calton Jail still stands in this picture taken in August 1936, but the rest of the prison has gone.

A train driver's view of the Caledonian Station taken in the 1950s. It has all gone now to make way for new roads, hotels and eventually a conference centre.

Construction work goes on at the junction of Princes Street and South Charlotte Street in the mid-1920s.

It looks like a film set, but it is a portrait of 19th-century Edinburgh in front of the site for the Usher Hall. The work of the pavement artist is coming in for a lot of admiration.

Shopping, 1950s style, in a shoe shop in Princes Street in 1958.

Market Street in 1960 looking west after the rush of early-morning business was over.

Market Street comes to a halt in June 1954. The fruit market was situated here until the mid-1960s and a bus garage at the far end added to the traffic turmoil. The North Bridge is seen at the top of the picture carrying the road across the valley of the old Nor' Loch, now the Waverley station.

Market Street again in the late 1950s, looking east.

In 1854 the Waverley station was not what it is today. Market Street is on the left of the picture and in the distance on the top right can be seen the National Gallery.

The railway takes over. In this 1960s picture the extent of the expansion of the Waverley can be seen. In the centre is what was the North British Hotel, now renamed the Balmoral, and on the skyline on the right is Nelson's Column.

The Calton Hill in 1905. The buildings are the Observatory partly designed by Playfair, the monument to philosopher Dugald Stewart, also by Playfair, the National Monument, often called the National Disgrace because it was never finished, and the Nelson monument.

The 1950s and Edinburgh is laid out for inspection. The Mound leads directly from the Royal Mile to Princes Street at the top of the picture, with the Gardens to the left. On the right is the rear of the National Gallery.

Winter comes to the West End around 1905.

Maule's Corner at the West End around the turn of the century.

A 1920s fashion show, again at the West End, while the models are waiting for a tram.

Just outside the grounds of Holyrood Palace at the foot of the Royal Mile, around 1900.

Allan Ramsay, the poet, lived here in the High Street from 1711 to 1725. This picture was taken at the turn of the century.

The Scott Monument in Princes Street Gardens late last century. A magnificent structure to just one of the capital's famous men of literature.

Winter in the Royal Botanic Garden.

Around 1880 the foot of North Bridge at the East End of Princes Street looked like this. The grandeur of the North British Hotel was yet to come.

The spire of the Tron Kirk stands over this 1950s picture of the South Bridge. Peter Allan is one of the many department stores to have disappeared since then.

Gracious living prefab style. This was one of the early ones to arrive in Edinburgh.

Stockbridge, one of the capital's early suburbs, now virtually in the city centre, in the 1950s.

Advocate's Close as it looked in 1884 before demolition and rebuilding.

It is washing day in an Edinburgh tenement.

Princes Street in the early 1950s.

South Edinburgh

Nicolson Street on a quiet morning before the buildings were upgraded.

The Union Canal at Craiglockhart. Edinburgh University rowing club uses this stretch of water.

June 1962 and Morningside Road is quiet. Quiet enough for someone to do a U-turn . . .or is he just parked there?

The view from the Royal Infirmary. A timeless picture. George Heriot's School in the centre has been there for 300 years, the Castle at top left, for even longer.

In the 1950s and '60s the Barbecue in Forrest Road was the meeting place . . .and being across the road from Edinburgh University Medical School it was never short of customers.

Bonfire night in the Grassmarket in 1952.

The top of Morrison Street as it will never be seen again. This was 1962. All the buildings have now gone, including the cycle shop.

The top of Church Hill, looking down Morningside Road at the turn of the century. Cable cars and horse-drawn carts were still the best transport available.

The road to Liberton was not much more than a mud track at the turn of the century.

George Square was elegant and very Georgian. It had character and beauty, but all that had to take second place when Edinburgh University started a massive expansion in the 1970s. Now the square lies at the heart of the university.

But George Square did not go under without protest . . .

The University expanded in all directions. This is how the Bristo area looked in the 1960s. Nothing remains. Even Parkers Stores, mum's delight, had to give way.

Tenements with a touch of class in Warrender Park Road early in the century.

Some change was sad, some was not. This area of St Leonard's was crying out for demolition when this picture was taken in the 1920s.

Arthur Street, in the shadow of Arthur's Seat, was really quite famous, the buildings were so poor and living conditions so bad. It has all been replaced by modern homes.

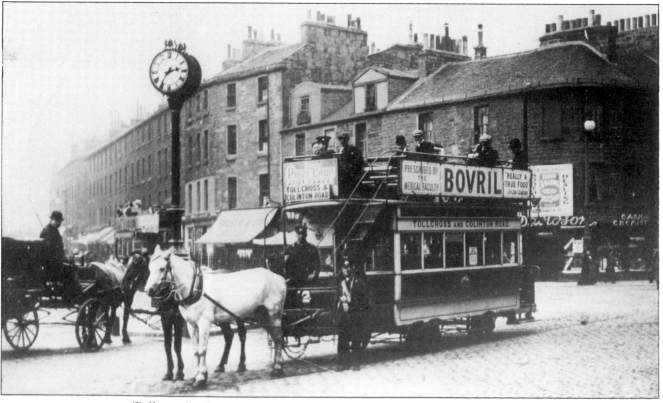

Tollcross late last century and the horse tram waits for the photographer.

Tollcross, again at the turn of the century.

The trams have changed, but in 1952 Tollcross had not changed much.

It's playtime at the foot of Victoria Street, dancing to the tune of the organ grinder.

It is 1908, and adults as well as children are captivated by the street ventriloquist.

Showboat comes to the Empire Theatre in the 1920s. The theatre is now being rebuilt as an opera house.

The story of Greyfriar's Bobby is known all over the world. His statue stands at the junction of Candlemaker Row and George IV Bridge, just outside Greyfriar's Churchyard where he watched over the grave of his master.

Parkers Stores again, and here the university buildings are already towering over their neighbours.

J.Turnbull and Sons were very proud of their van when they took delivery of it early this century.

All the buildings on the left of Earl Gray Street have gone to make way for modern developments.

Hustle, bustle and lots of waiting when Blyth's department store held a sale in the 1960s.

Inside Blyth's in the 1950s there was an oasis of calm in the tea room.

Delivery time at L.Laurenson, the wine and spirit merchants in Leith at the beginning of the century.

Deacon Brodie was a respected citizen by day. By night he was a thief. And this is where he ended up, in the graveyard of Buccleuch Parish Church, after the hangman had finished with him.

When James Goldsmith and Miss Maria Isabel Patino eloped to Scotland to be married it became headline news. Her father, a Bolivian tin-mining millionaire pursued them and tried to stop the marriage. In Edinburgh, they stayed with friends at Prestonfield House, then a private home. Here, it is under siege by the Press in January 1954.

High School Wynd late last century, so called because the original High School, now part of the university, was situated at the top.

North Edinburgh

Plumbing was sometimes a bit primitive. This was Leith in the early 1920s.

The Shore in Leith, where the Water of Leith runs under the bridge into the dock area.

The fishing fleet at Newhaven harbour in 1936.

Playtime in the streets and a group of children look to their leader.

The Kirkgate in Leith in the 1950s. There was nowhere else quite like it for shops of all sorts.

Another view of the Kirkgate which has been replaced in the redevelopment of Leith.

The Shore in Leith and a two masted sailing vessel and a paddle steamer are alongside in 1858.

Musselburgh at the turn of the century, and the Town House doesn't have to contend with much traffic.

The top of Leith Street was always dominated by Littlejohns, the bakers, now gone in the redevelopment.

Outside toilets and TV aerials. This was West Close in Newhaven in 1966 — and yet, close by were modern flats.

Portobello in the 1960s.

Portobello in the 1950s, and the angry sea is bursting over the promenade.

The fleet's in . . .and the fish market is open at Newhaven around 1900.

Washing day in a quiet corner of Dean Village in 1960.

The old Cramond Brig that led over the River Almond to Queensferry around 1873.

Barnton Gardens, in the early part of the century. An exclusive suburb where cars and horses mingled happily.

Early this century and ships line the quayside on the Shore at Leith, with the Commercial Street bridge in the background.

In 1952 this was the main road from Leith to Granton. Now the centre of Newhaven is bypassed and modern homes have replaced many of the older buildings.

Trams, buses, cars and people jostle in Leith Street in the 1950s before the building of the St James Centre. It was a street of shops, pubs, dance halls and snooker rooms, that hardly ever slept.

Delivering the goods at the beginning of this century. A housewife picks up her shopping at the end of Cumberland Street.

St Stephen's Church in the 1930s.

Before the days of the Forth Road Bridge the ferry at Queensferry was a vital link between Fife and the south. Here the last ferry, a blaze of lights, casts off in the lee of the railway bridge. The date was February 1958.

Off to the Steamie! Before washing machines were a fixture in most homes, the public wash houses provided a much-needed service. They were more than simply places where the family clothes were cleaned. They were also a gathering place, where women could exchange gossip.

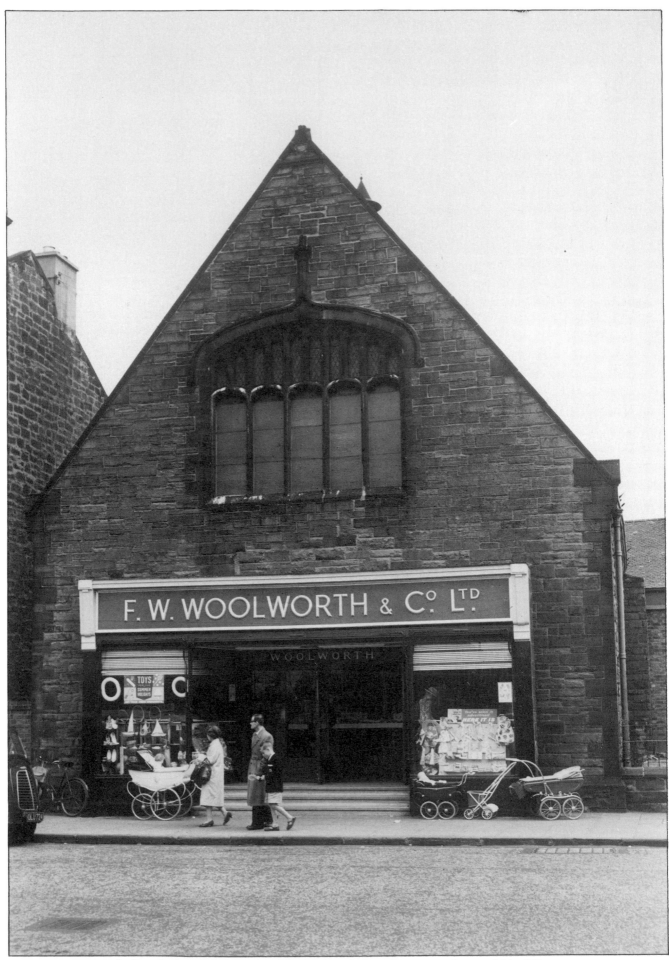

In Portobello High Street in 1962 Woolworth found a new use for an old building.

The ferries were still plying their trade on the Forth, but their days were numbered in 1959 as the beginnings of the Forth Road Bridge appear.

Stockbridge in the 1960s. The bridge over the Water of Leith is a far cry from the original wooden one.

Leith docks . . .a scene from the 1960s.

High living in Muirhouse.

Register House at the bottom left gets into the picture with Leith Street before the massive redevelopment of the 1960s which brought New St Andrew's House and the St James Centre and swept away a part of Edinburgh's history.

The Dean Bridge and beyond it a part of Dean Village.

West Edinburgh

Dial 28 for service with a smile. Your order would be delivered by van or by bike from Weierter's in Corstorphine without delay, earlier this century.

The country village look has gone, replaced by a modern medical centre, but otherwise, Ladywell Road in Corstorphine has retained its old fashioned charm.

St John's Road, Corstorphine, around 1900. Then, this was an outlying suburb. Today, it is one of the city's busiest roads.

When horses ruled the roads, the blacksmith was king. This is the old 'smiddy' at Corstorphine taken about 1900.

Almost 400 years old, this sycamore tree in Corstorphine carries a legend of passion and murder. Christian Nimmo and her lover, James, Laird of Forrester, met there secretly, until one night they had a terrible row, and she pulled his sword from its scabbard and killed him. She was found guilty and beheaded on 12 November 1679. It is said her ghost still wanders near the tree, dressed in white.

St John's Road, Corstorphine, still recognisable after about 80 years.

There have been few changes in Colinton village since the early part of the century, but the village atmosphere has been submerged in the rush of traffic.

Inglis Green cottages at Slateford in the early 1900s.

Slateford village grew up on the banks of the Water of Leith. It was a major crossing point for travellers from the west. It is still that today, but new roads and roundabouts have changed the scene dramatically.

Haymarket is one of the city's busiest intersections. Many plans have been tried to control the flow of traffic. This was one of them in 1954.

In 1908 the Scottish National Exhibition was held in Saughton Park. The fun and games on the helter skelter fascinated most of the crowd, but one man and a boy found the photographer more interesting.

It took Edinburgh quite a long time to get its modern airport. Until then it had to make do. This was the old airport in 1956.

Edinburgh People

James Bond at home with his mum and dad and the family dog. Sean Connery never forgets his roots in Edinburgh. This was 1962.

The roots: The year was 1936 and James Bond was a long way into the future, but Tam Connery was one of the boys at Bruntsfield Primary School.

Ronald Corbett, it says on the back of the photograph. This was before he became better known to everyone as Ronnie.

Roy Thomson, later Lord Thomson of Fleet, took over The Scotsman Publications in the early 1950s. Here he surveys the new look *Scotsman* which had gone over to front page news. It was 17 April 1957.

Roy Rogers and Trigger came to town and they stayed at the Caledonian Hotel. Well, Roy Rogers did. Trigger stayed at the St Cuthbert's Co-op stables. But on this occasion he had visited Roy in his hotel room. In fact there were two Triggers. The stage act was so demanding that it was one show per horse daily.

Family life around 1900. But which family? The picture was found in a building being demolished.

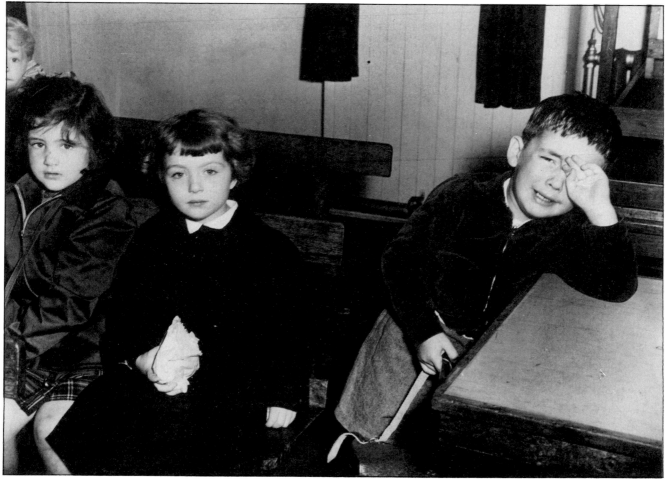

Nerves on the first day at school. Norman Briggs protests loudly in August 1954.

There were almost riots in the streets when the Beatles came to town in 1964.

Gene Kelly danced into town in April, 1953. Here he is with his producer Arthur Freed at the Caledonian Hotel.

Prince Charles had a boyish look when he visited the *Evening News* office in the early 1970s. Behind him is the then editor Max McAuslane.

Actor Duncan Macrae serving up meals to a group of ladies in 1956. It was the opening of the old peoples' lunch club, in Cables Wynd, Leith.

A smile from Festival visitor Richard Burton in 1953. With him are Claire Bloom and, on his left, Fay Compton.

A welcoming crowd gathers to see Orson Welles in the 1950s.

Edinburgh Childhood

In February 1952, there were ten sets of twins at St Cuthbert's School. Here, teacher Mr H.Bocker is pictured with a class of them.

August 1955, and it is the first day at Tollcross Primary school for a group of five-year-olds.

Everyone is paying a lot of attention to what is going on in the corner at South Morningside school in January 1956.

It's a fair cop! And Brian Pithie takes a note of everything that has been going on in South Fort Street, Leith, in 1957.

Smile please, it's time for fun in the sun at Portobello in July 1958.

More fun in the sun . . .this time it is North Berwick, Edinburgh's favourite seaside resort.

All set for a boat trip at North Berwick at the beginning of the century.

A class photograph from 1885. This was Castle Hill school.

It was a cold winter in 1956, and that gave the opportunity for skating on the Union Canal.

Pitch and toss, barefoot, in the street in 1909.

Abbey Strand and the entrance to Holyrood Palace. Here, before 1880, debtors could find sanctuary from the law.

Having your haircut in Patrick Thomson's was an experience many children had to endure. But it was made more acceptable because of the selection of rocking horses. It probably did not make the hairdresser's job any easier.

The film showing was *The Royal Marriage,* the film of the wedding of King George VI, but it drew the crowds of children to the penny matinee at the Picturedrome in Easter Road in 1923.

Gifford Park in November 1929. The streets were the only playground.

Rocking horses are always a favourite. This was the Jamaica Street Children's Playroom in 1954.

Cookery classes at Portobello High School in 1953.

The old schoolhouse in Morningside in 1923. The building has been preserved, and the clock, which for many years stood at 3.40, is back in service.

St Margaret's Loch in Holyrood Park in 1957, when boating in the sun was one of life's little pleasures.

...Or if you didn't have a boat handy, you could walk into the water.

A 'Collie Buckie' fight in Tron Square in 1954.

Christmas 1958 in the toy department of Thornton's.

Hula hoops forever in the backgreens of Marchmont in April, 1957.

Down to the sea in ships . . .or in this case to Inverleith pond with a sloop-rigged model yacht during the summer of 1954.

A game of marbles attracts an admiring crowd in 1955.

"It is time to come in for your tea . . .". Mum lays down the law in a back court in Sciennes in 1959.

The race is over and it is time for repairs.

Time for Play

Canoeing on the Union Canal at Viewforth in July 1957.

The winners receive their prizes at one of the beauty contests at the Palais de Danse in Fountainbridge. This was May 1959.

Miss Lambretta gets on her bike in October 1958.

Also in October 1958, the Mazda Queen of Light was switched on.

There's something about the tartan . . .this was August 1956 at the entrance to Edinburgh Castle.

Chipperfield's Circus comes to town and the camels parade along Princes Street in 1955.

Edinburgh Zoo is famous for its penguin colony. Here it is spring cleaning time in April, 1960.

It's 'All aboard the Skylark,' in July 1957 at Portobello. But judging by the dress, it was a cold day to be at the seaside.

Cramond Beach in August, 1958, and it is still chilly.

Cramond harbour in the 1950s, and all sails are set . . .

Portobello beach at the turn of the century, showing the pier that is long gone.

Edinburgh is the home of golf. James VI of Scotland took the game to England when he became James I. There are 28 golf courses in the city. Bruntsfield Links was one of the early ones, although now it is a pitch and putt course. This was the scene there in 1870.

Portobello in 1908, with the old Pier.

The donkeys get down to some serious business.

About 50 years separate these pictures of Portobello beach, but nothing much has changed except the clothing. They are still eating gritty sandwiches, digging holes and building sand castles. The dates: around the turn of the century and July 1950.

A group of young people posing for the camera below Portobello pier at the beginning of the century.

August 1954 — the early days of stock car racing at Meadowbank.

Edinburgh at War

BRITAIN ORDERS COMPLETE MOBILISATION

King Signs Orders at Privy Council Meeting

The German Onslaught

TOWNS BOMBED

Many Casualties in Warsaw

GERMAN ATTACKS "ON ALL FRONTIERS"

Reich Navy "Takes Over" the Baltic

TREATY INVOKED

Poland Asks Britain for Her Aid

A.R.P. WARNINGS IN OPERATION

Mobilisation and "State of Siege" in France

THE DAY'S EVENTS IN BRIEF

KEEP CALM

STATE THE LORD PROVOST AND TREASURER

MEDIATION OFFER

FRANCE REPLIES TO DUCE'S PROPOSAL

SPECIAL EDITION TO-NIGHT

LEAGUE COMMISSIONER LEAVES DANZIG

BELGIAN MOBILISATION

HARVEST HELPERS WANTED

DUKE OF WINDSOR COMING HOME?

PARLIAMENT TO-NIGHT

FRENCH DECREES

ROOSEVELT'S APPEAL

FRENCH DECREES

A.R.P. ARRANGEMENTS

EIRE COUNCIL MEETS

PAINTINGS REMOVED

LONDON SAYS POLAND JUSTIFIED

THE PRIVY COUNCIL

KING SIGNS VITAL ORDERS

MEETING LASTS ONLY 12 MINUTES

"HUMILIATING POSITION"

GERMANS USING GAS?

CALL TO ARMS

POLISH PRESIDENT'S MESSAGE

PARLIAMENT TO MEET TO-NIGHT

Cabinet Session This Morning

CEASELESS COMINGS AND GOINGS

AN URGENT NEED

BLANKETS FOR EVACUATED CHILDREN

VISCOUNT GORT

Raid Warning System In Operation

OTHER NEWS OF TO-DAY

FIGHTING IN DANZIG

POLISH VERSION

BOMBER BROUGHT DOWN

TAKEN UNAWARES

TAKEN UNAWARES

BRITISH MOBILISATION

TREATY INVOKED

POLAND EXPECTS—

War was on the way. This is how the Evening News reported the state of the world on 1 September 1939.

A barrage balloon goes up at South Queensferry. The Forth Bridge was one of the early targets for the Luftwaffe.

. . .And this is what can happen to you if you try to bomb the Forth Bridge. The first German aircraft brought down over Britain in the Second World War. The credit goes to 603 (City of Edinburgh) Squadron, Auxiliary Air Force.

For you the war is over . . .another view of the Heinkel brought down in East Lothian.

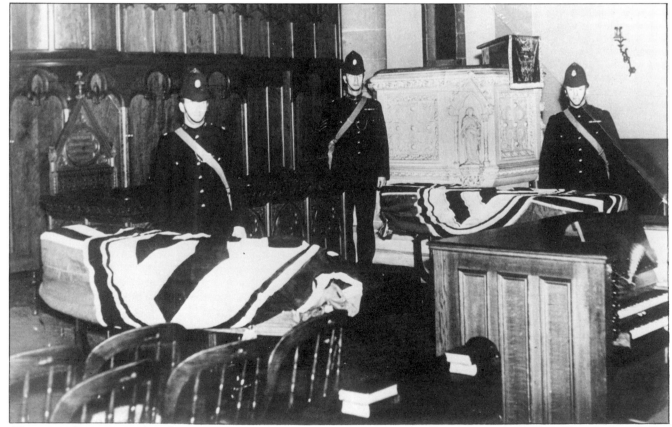

They were the enemy . . .but they were treated with respect. Bodies of German fliers lying at St Philip's Church, Portobello.

Princes Street, 1940, and an ME 109 is on display to launch a Fighting Planes Fund by the WVS.

A German pilot's eye view of Granton harbour.
This is a Luftwaffe map issued to pilots.

All clear, and time to leave the air-raid shelters in Princes Street Gardens.

It was claimed to be the world's biggest bomb, on display at RAF Turnhouse in 1946.

Anson bombers flying over the Forth Bridge. South Queensferry and its harbour can be seen below.

Battle of Britain Week 1957, and Hawker Hunters give a flying display at RAF Turnhouse.

Around and About

In January 1958, this train didn't stop at the old Caledonian Station . . not until it had smashed through the buffers and leaped onto the platform. No one was seriously injured.

It's time to go home, and workers at the North British Rubber Company at Fountainbridge are eager to catch their buses, some time in the 1950s.

The scene is the Old Quad at Edinburgh University, and they were making the film *Journey to the Centre of the Earth*. It was June 1959.

East Fortune, a wartime airfield, was pressed into service again in April 1961, when improvements were being made to the runway at Turnhouse. This was the renovated control tower.

April 1956, and Leith Docks was the point of departure for ten Centurion tanks destined for the Swedish armed forces.

Edinburgh was once alive with breweries. Rationalisation has meant that there are now fewer, but larger ones. This was Usher's, now only a memory, in 1957.

The Munrospun factory at Restalrig in the 1950s.

The opening ceremony of the Court of Session in October, 1954. Sir John Cameron, Dean of the Faculty, leads the advocates to St Giles.

Mick McGahey explaining why Scottish miners refused to go back to work until the sacked miners were reinstated after the strike. It was March 1985.

The Royal Bank of Scotland were on the move with their travelling branch office in 1956.

The old Edinburgh Airport, at Turnhouse in April 1956.

New technology started to rear its head at the *Evening News* office in 1982. Here, the hot-metal typesetters are being removed from the building. Photo typesetting had arrived.

The trams had gone off the rails, and this was the sad fate for many of them in October 1956.

November 1956, and the tram lines are being lifted from Princes Street.

A pony and an organ . . .that was entertainment, passing Tollcross in 1962.

Housewives share a gossip over a hot tub . . .washing day in Newhaven in the 1880s.

Whatever happened to clay pipes? They were big business in 1908 when this picture was taken at William Christie's factory in Leith.

A visitor from France . . .gets a welcome from the younger generation. An ''Onion Johnny'' in the city in the 1950s.

Banks, the pet shop in Fleshmarket Close was a city institution. It closed in the early 1980s when the two brothers who ran it decided to retire. Before that it had seemed to have been there for ever . . .

Even in the 1930s people got thirsty.

This shop in St Stephen Street sold almost everything: hooks and eyes, potted head, fireworks, Sunlight soap. And you could have your mangling done as well, around the turn of the century.

It started in the city tours . . .one-man buses, but then the driver had to don a ticket machine to collect the fares. Nowadays, of course, no one has heard of conductors.

Wellington boots were one of the prize products of the North British Rubber Company in the 1950s. And this is how they did it.

All set for action. The Fire Brigade at their Lauriston Place headquarters in 1930. Edinburgh's brigade is reputed to be the oldest in the country, being set up in 1824.

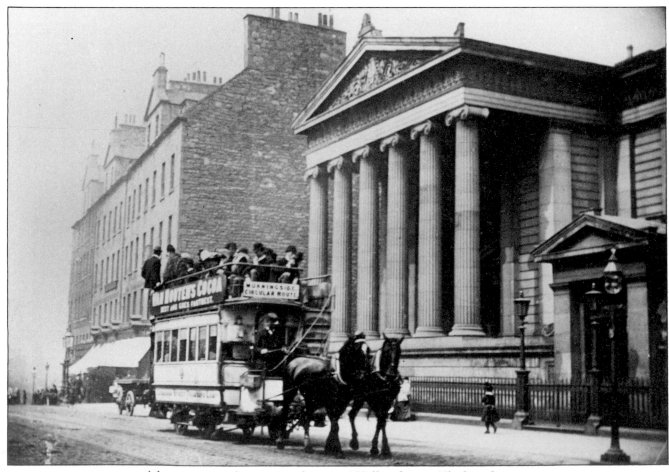

A horse tram on its way past Surgeons' Hall and on to Nicolson Street.

Milk in sealed bottles was something to shout about in 1925, and this dairy in Morrison Street did just that.

Buchan Pottery in Portobello in the 1950s. These girls were at work in the throwing room.

Buchan Pottery in 1923, and this was how the office staff went about their business.

St Patrick Square at the turn of the century. Cockels and mussels make a tasty meal.

It is all mechanised now, but this is how they once cleaned the streets. And the 'Scaffies' took a lot of pride in their work.

The Fisher Howard cork cutting factory in Leith stops for a moment to let the photographer do his stuff.

The foot of Leith Walk in 1904 . . .and gangs of workmen lay the new tram lines.

Princes Street at the turn of the century. A gang of workmen are digging up the pavements.

It seemed a good idea at the time . . .During the First World War experiments were made with running buses on coal gas. The bus had to carry a bag of gas on the roof filled with the fuel. This one is standing on Waverley Bridge.

The Mound was given an electric blanket during the 1950s. Ice and snow would no longer be a hazard. It lasted only a short time. Persistent faults pushed the costs too high.

Repairs to the tramlines in Princes Street in 1953.

Hot off the presses the newspapers were delivered to trains and newsagents. This was the Scotsman Publications fleet of vans lined up in Market Street in 1948.

The Forth Bridge has been the setting for many a drama. This was the filming of *The Thirty Nine Steps* on 29 September 1958. Star of the film, Kenneth More, is pointing to the camera.

It's the pits for Darkie, the pony being fed by miner David Gilfillan in 15 October 1958.

Darkie at work.

The Scottish National Fat Stock Show at Waverley Market in December 1959.

Hot water bottles from the North British Rubber Company being given a hand-painted touch of class in 1958.

Martin's of Frederick Street were the experts in making fishing tackle. This scene is from September 1957.

Busy lines all round for the telephone exchange girls in 1955.

A parade by Leith unemployed workers' club around 1937 passes up the Hig

treet in an appeal for funds for the Royal Infirmary.

This was St Ninian's Row, the main street in the old Barony of Calton. It was demolished in 1844.

The Royal Infirmary Pageant in the 1930s, passes through Holyrood Park.

The East End in 1953. On the left, the Palace Cinema and Woolworth's have now gone.

The legend says "Heave awa' chaps, I'm no' dead yet." It is above the entrance to Paisley Close in the High Street and commemorates the disaster on 24 November, 1861, when the front of a tenement building collapsed. During the rescue work a boy, Joseph McIver, shouted the now immortalised quotation to his struggling rescuers.

June 1939 — and the French battleship
Dunkerque arrives . . .war was only a
whisper away.

The liner *SS Mauretania* arrives in the
Forth. She came to be broken up.

The American battleship *USS Iowa* arrives for a courtesy call in 1957.

Early in World War Two, the battleship *HMS Rodney* pays a visit to the Forth.

The fleet's in port, and *HMS Implacable* lies at anchor near the Forth Bridge in the early 1950s.

This etching shows how tightly cramped was the High Street in the days when the Tolbooth stood alongside St Giles.
It was finally pulled down in 1817.

SUBSCRIBERS

PRESENTATION COPY
The City of Edinburgh

1 Kenneth E Walker
2 Anton C Rippon
3 Nicola J Rippon
4 Graham A Hales
5 Philip J Southall
6 Julia E Gray
7 John L Peat
8 D R McIntosh
9 Mr J Hamilton
10 Mrs Doreen Milliken
11 Phyllis Edmonstone
12 Robert W Gilchrist
13 George L Allan
14 John Liddle
15 K R McIntyre
16 John Moore
17 I S Haigh
18 Isobel Ross
19 S J Ward
20 Bruce Wilson
21 M Mackay
22 Gillian M Headspeath
23 John B Black
24 A R Macdonald
25 Jim & May Lindsay
26 Brida B Jones
27 Brida B Jones
28 Robert H Cranston
29 Mr W Murray
30 Douglas M Campbell
31 Senior Librarian, Main
   City Library,
   Edinburgh
32 Niel Anderson
33 Niel Anderson
34 Mrs C Gent
35 Kenneth B Wilson
36 Helen D Piechniczek
37 H McKenna
38 Mrs Margeret R King
39 Karen A Esson
40 Mrs Jean Dickson
41 D McCulloch
42 Kenny Harris

43 Terry Thomson
44 M & B Wilkinson
45 Margaret Munro
46 Hugh Kemp
47 Kathleen Ferguson
48 Ian Bremner
49 Alexander Davie
50 John Gray
51 Ian Ramsay
52 Frances M Rennie
53 Mrs M A Allen
54 Mrs L Rafferty
55 C B Lenaghen
56 C B Lenaghen
57 Michael & Sheila
   Moncrieff, Auckland,
   New Zealand
58 Kenneth & Christine
   MacDonald, Auld
   Reekie
59 Malcolm Burt
60 Frances A C Young
61 Archie M Wilson
62 William Gray
63 Fraser Birrell
64 Sheila Anderson
65 Gloria M Keeney
66 Mr P Houston
67 Mr P Houston
68 T K Stafford
69 Gavin C Lunn
70 J Doctor
71 Mr James W Buckle
72 Fraser J Morrison
73 Mr Hector Jackson
74 Stephen James Hogg
75 Mr Peter V Cassidy
76 Robert Sewell
77 Peter Berg
78 Mr & Mrs Ross McInnes
79 Douglas A Glass
80 Iain & Anne Macdonald
81 W Bradbury
82 Elizabeth F Payne

83 K Pollard
84 Cathrine M White
85 Sandra M Smith
86 Mrs A F Ramsay
87 Ian A Muir
88 Eileen Irvine
89 J Lundius
90 John Miller
91 S Robertson
92 Mrs J Harris
93 J Heatlie
94 E H Stein
95 Dennis R Meadows
96 H J Martin
97 Mrs J R Punton
98 Harold & Peggy
   Wilkening
99 Mrs Mary Ann Wilson
100 James Cheyne
101 Ernest J Mullen
102 James M MacKenzie
103 FR J Nicholson
104 Malcolm Cant
105 Douglas Welsh
106 Evelyn A Hutchison
107 Fiona Porteous
108 Stanley Moodie
109 John Charles Watling
110 Mrs A M Walker
111 Mr Robert Heron
112 Scott Miller
113 Robert S Forbes
114 Ronald Sutherland
115 Robert Muir
116 Ron Thomson
117 M Godfrey
118 Helen Gibson
119 Douglas R F Pearson
120 Ian C Ross
121 William G Menzies
122 Miss M A Laidlaw
123 Angus Robert Swan
124 Betty Brown
125 Brian Coulson

126 Ian Scott
127 Mrs Ray Wright
128 Mrs Hilda Thomson
129 Jean Abel
130 Mrs A Baird
131 Gerry
132 A Boswell
133 Thomas S Torrance
134 E C Waugh
135 Andrew Watt
136 G Gillespie
137 Mr J L Hogarth
138 Ronnie Garrett
139 Sarah Ross
140 Mary Bryce Lockhart
141 Mary Jacomb
142 Peter W Gillam
143 George Blyth
144 John Rutherford
145 Alasdair B Quinney
146 Ron Ross
147 Robert Thomson
148 G Kunze
149 James B N McCafferty
150 R Falconer
151 Marion Paris
152 John Stanyard
153 Wallace M Beattie
154 Elaine Mahon
155 Jean M Welsh
156 William Innes Murray
157 Tom Inglis
158 Jacqueline McColl
159 Graham Sutherland
    Main
160 Robert Sutherland
161 William Watson
162 Isabella W Hardie
163 R W Syme
164 Robert Ferguson
165 James Dickson
166 Peter J Campbell Smith
167 Peter Glasgow
168 Dr James Nally
169 Mr & Mrs C W Cook
170 Ellen Cameron
171 Willie Bruce
172 Andrew Sinclair
173 Robert Scott
174 Mabel M McGill
175 Lewis Simpson
176 Mr Edgar Deighton
177 Mr Edgar Deighton

178 W P Florence
179 Multiflex
180 Marion MacDonald
181 Frank A Sibbald
182 Mrs June Henderson
183 Mrs June Henderson
184 Alastair Ormiston
185 R Davidson
186 R Davidson
187 Emma J Liddle
188 E M Melville
189 Ying C Bygate
190 Ying C Bygate
191 Mr & Mrs A W Heath
192 Ruth A Mills
193 Mrs Betty Broom
194 Mrs Jill Pelosi
195 Eileen Philips
196 John Love
197 D R Robertson
198 Alan Mair
199 Alan Mair
200 John J Gunn
201 The Revd Alasdair Elders
202 Hugh Brodie
203 Colin Pope
204 Geraldine McPhee
205 Mrs H Barr
206 David Fleming-Miller
207 Ronald Robb
208 Mary Jane Meldrum
209 A E Heron
210 John G Carbray
211 Peter F Lawrence
212 John Ross
213 Agnes McFarlane
214 Mrs I A Greig
215 Roy MacConnachie
216 Carol Elliott
217 Mrs J Weir
218 John Laurie Scott
219 Gordon S Paterson
220 Stuart Horsburgh
221 Robert Wyllie
222 Gary Thorburn
223 Peter S Reid
224 John Bambery
225 Ann Berczuk
226 Ralph Fusco
227 A Fisher
228 W A Russell
229 Richard Grahame
230 Stanley Smith

231 Thomas Malcolm
232 Dorothy Waugh
233 Christopher B Reekie
234 Robert S Nelson
235 Mary Brown
236 David M Y McGill
237 Mr G Evans
238 Dennis W Harvey
239 Beatrice Morrison
240 David J Jacobs
241 Brian A Wishart
242 E R Bullen
243 Robin Wallace
244 Mr John W Stewart
245 Peter McIntyre
246 Christine Hogg
247 Gerry & Amy